CORAL

A Buddy Book by
Deborah Coldiron

ABDO
Publishing Company

UNDERWATER
WORLD

VISIT US AT
www.abdopublishing.com

Published by ABDO Publishing Company, 8000 West 78th Street, Edina, Minnesota 55439.

Copyright © 2008 by Abdo Consulting Group, Inc. International copyrights reserved in all countries. No part of this book may be reproduced in any form without written permission from the publisher. Buddy Books™ is a trademark and logo of ABDO Publishing Company.

Printed in the United States.

Coordinating Series Editor: Sarah Tieck
Contributing Editor: Michael P. Goecke
Graphic Design: Deborah Coldiron
Cover Photograph: Photos.com
Interior Photographs/Illustrations: Animals Animals - Earth Scenes: E.R. Degginger (page 19), Peter Harrison/OSF (page 17); Art Explosion (pages 7, 15, 22, 28); Clipart.com (page 9); Brandon Cole Marine Photography (pages 11, 13); Corbis (page 11); ImageMix (page 13); Minden Pictures: Fred Bavendam (pages 25, 27), Flip Nicklin (page 29), D.P. Wilson/FLPA (page 23); Photodisc (page 19); Photos.com (pages 5, 7, 18, 19, 21, 30)

Library of Congress Cataloging-in-Publication Data

Coldiron, Deborah.
    Coral / Deborah Coldiron.
      p. cm. — (Underwater world)
    Includes index.
    ISBN 978-1-59928-811-6
    1. Coral reef animals—Juvenile literature. 2. Coral reef biology—Juvenile literature. I. Title.

QL125.C64 2008
578.77'89—dc22

2007017852

Table Of Contents

The World Of Coral

Every living creature needs water. Some animals not only need water, they live in it, too.

Scientists have found more than 250,000 kinds of plants and animals living underwater. And, they believe there could be one million more! Coral is one animal that makes its home in this underwater world.

Seventy percent of Earth's surface is covered in water.

Corals are small creatures. Often, they live together in groups called colonies.

Individual corals are called polyps. The smallest polyps are less than one-sixteenth of an inch (.2 cm) in size. But, some coral polyps can grow as large as 12 inches (30 cm).

There are thousands of coral **species** in our underwater world. Corals are found in oceans all over Earth. Some live in shallow coastal waters. Others live in waters up to 20,000 feet (6,000 m) deep!

FAST FACTS Corals first appeared in Earth's oceans more than 500 million years ago.

There is a wide variety of shapes, colors, and species of coral in the underwater world.

Get A Little Closer

An individual coral polyp has a tube-shaped body. It looks like a small **sea anemone**. A coral polyp has **tentacles** on its top end. And, it attaches its underside to other living or dead polyps.

Many coral polyps live in colonies. But some do not. These polyps attach to hard surfaces on the seafloor.

FAST FACTS

Some corals have very rough surfaces! Divers can get nasty scrapes if they get too close.

The Body Of A Coral Polyp

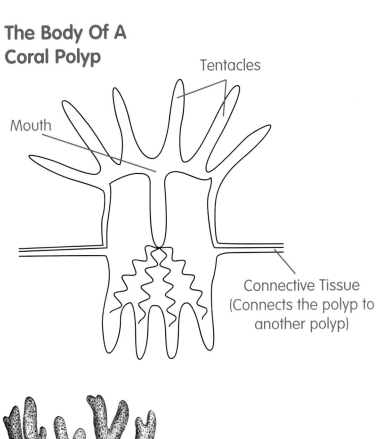

Tentacles

Mouth

Connective Tissue
(Connects the polyp to
another polyp)

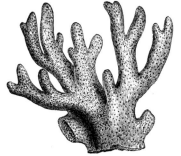

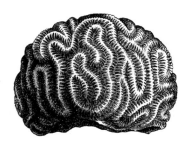

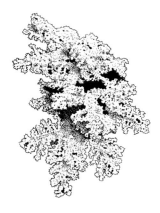

Individual coral polyps may form
colonies of different shapes.

There are a wide variety of coral colonies. They can take many different shapes.

Brain coral forms a smooth, **spherical** mound. Finger coral is made up of many spiky branches. Pillar coral looks like a group of columns. And, cabbage coral looks like a head of cabbage.

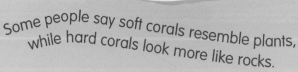

Some people say soft corals resemble plants, while hard corals look more like rocks.

Brain Coral

Cabbage Coral

The two basic types of coral are hard and soft. Hard corals are more common and familiar than soft corals.

Hard corals build reefs. They develop tough outer skeletons. When the coral polyps die, their skeletons remain. These skeletons form a base on which reefs grow.

Soft corals are **flexible** and grow more quickly than hard corals. Instead of a hard skeleton, soft corals have tiny hard crystals throughout their bodies.

FAST FACTS

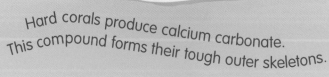

Hard corals produce calcium carbonate. This compound forms their tough outer skeletons.

Hard Coral

Soft Coral

Growing Coral

Corals reproduce in different ways. A coral colony may increase in size through the "budding" of individual polyps. Or, a new colony may be started through **spawning**.

When corals bud, individual polyps produce new polyps. When they reach a certain size, the buds detach from the parent polyp. Then, the new polyp attaches itself to the colony. This helps the colony grow.

Like most other corals, orange cup coral polyps can reproduce in more than one way.

Corals also reproduce by **spawning**. They release eggs, which are then **fertilized**. These fertilized eggs develop into larvae. The larvae swim to new locations to begin new colonies.

Sometimes new colonies form from existing colonies. This happens when pieces break off and drift away.

Entire colonies often spawn together on the same night. The normally clear waters around the reef become filled with tiny fertilized eggs.

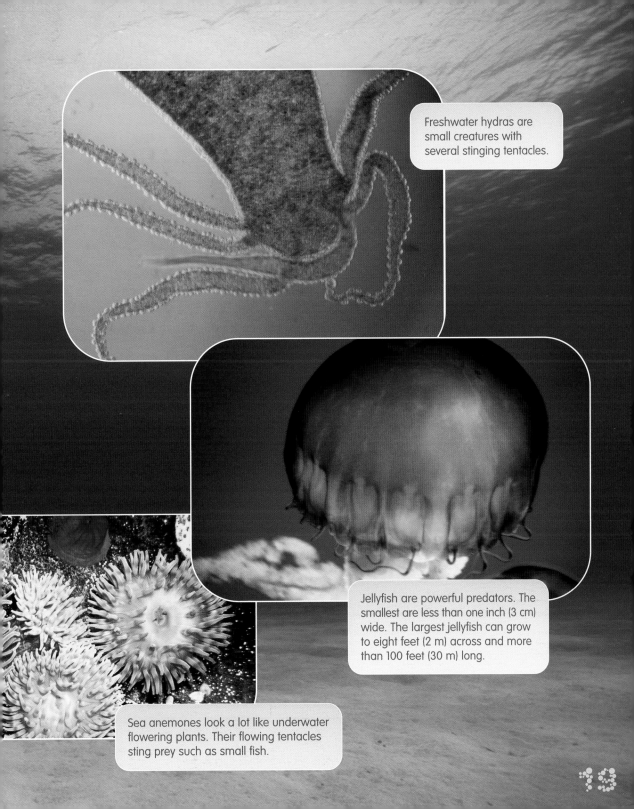

Freshwater hydras are small creatures with several stinging tentacles.

Jellyfish are powerful predators. The smallest are less than one inch (3 cm) wide. The largest jellyfish can grow to eight feet (2 m) across and more than 100 feet (30 m) long.

Sea anemones look a lot like underwater flowering plants. Their flowing tentacles sting prey such as small fish.

In The Neighborhood

Coral reefs are populated by a wide variety of ocean life. About 4,000 **species** of fish live in coral reefs. So do other sea animals, such as **crustaceans**.

Corals have a long list of neighbors. This group includes butterfly fish, sea snakes, sea horses, and moray eels. There are also octopuses, **sea anemones**, and sponges living among corals.

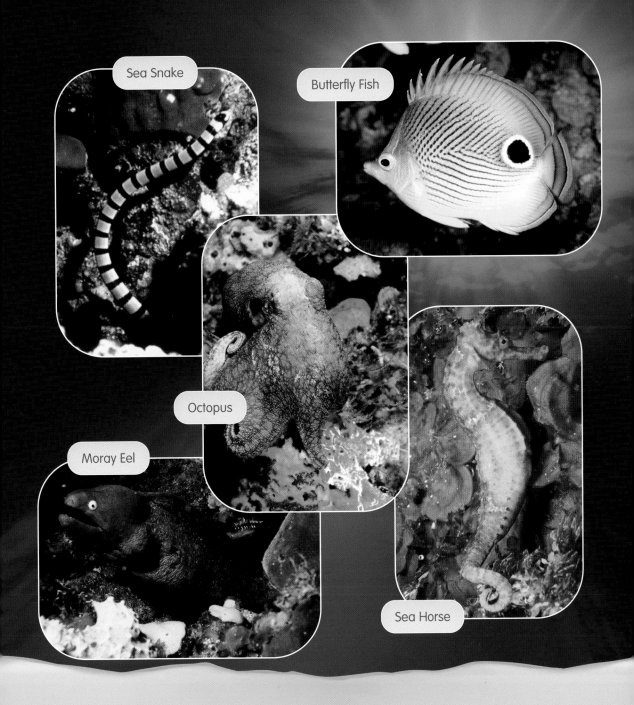

Sea Snake

Butterfly Fish

Octopus

Moray Eel

Sea Horse

Picky Eaters

Corals extend their tentacles into the water to catch food.

Corals often feed on plankton. To catch these tiny plants and animals, the coral polyps extend stinging **tentacles** into the water.

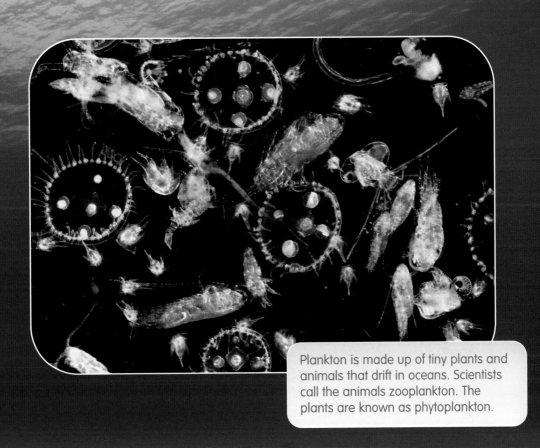

Plankton is made up of tiny plants and animals that drift in oceans. Scientists call the animals zooplankton. The plants are known as phytoplankton.

Corals feed most actively during the night. But during the day, many reef-building corals receive **nutrients** from zooxanthellae (zoh-uh-zan-THUH-lee). These are single-celled **algae** plants.

These tiny plants live inside the coral polyps. The polyps feed on some of the algae's waste products. The algae also make use of some of the polyps' waste. This relationship is called symbiosis.

Reef-building corals, such as hard corals, are hosts to zooxanthellae. Most corals get their color from the algae living inside them.

A Sensitive Species

Coral reefs are very sensitive. Small changes in temperature can threaten their health. Also, pollution is a growing problem.

Balance is important to a reef's health, too. If water is too rich in **nutrients**, **algae** multiply quickly. Then, too many algae overpower the coral.

Some animals, such as the crown-of-thorns starfish, eat corals. So do some fish. These include parrot fish, butterfly fish, and tangs.

FAST FACTS

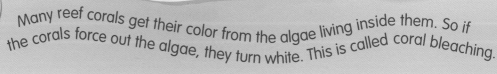

Many reef corals get their color from the algae living inside them. So if the corals force out the algae, they turn white. This is called coral bleaching.

When coral polyps are stressed, they force out the algae living inside them. If the stress stops, the corals will recover and let the algae back in. But if the stress continues, the corals will die. They leave behind hard, white skeletons.

Fascinating Facts

ian Coral

🪸 Some types of coral are desirable to jewelry makers. Gorgonian corals are known for their red coloring. They are often called "precious corals."

🪸 Instead of living in colonies, some corals live alone. The largest **solitary** coral polyps can grow up to 12 inches (30 cm) wide!

🪸 The world's largest coral reef is the Great Barrier Reef. It is located off the northeastern coast of Australia. Around 400 **species** of coral can be found in this large reef system. The entire reef covers 135,000 square miles (350,000 sq km) of the ocean floor.

Great Barrier Reef

Learn And Explore

Coral can be a good substitute for human bone! Sometimes, people's bones are destroyed by tumors, injuries, or infections. Doctors can use **porous** coral as a framework to grow new bone.

Hard coral skeletons have many tiny holes, like a sponge. This is good for growing human bone.

IMPORTANT WORDS

alga a plant or plant-like organism that lives mainly in water.

crustacean any of a group of animals with hard shells that live mostly in water. Crabs, lobsters, and shrimp are all crustaceans.

fertile able to produce seeds, fruit, or young.

flexible a tough, but bendable, material.

nutrient a substance that living beings take in for growth and development.

porous having tiny spaces or holes that allow fluids or air to pass through.

sea anemone an attached marine animal with stinging tentacles around its mouth opening.

solitary alone.

spawning the release of eggs.

species living things that are very much alike.

spherical sphere shaped, such as a globe or a baseball.

tentacle a long, slender body part that grows around the mouth or head of some animals.

WEB SITES

To learn more about coral, visit ABDO Publishing Company on the World Wide Web. Web sites about coral are featured on our Book Links page. These links are routinely monitored and updated to provide the most current information available.

www.abdopublishing.com

INDEX